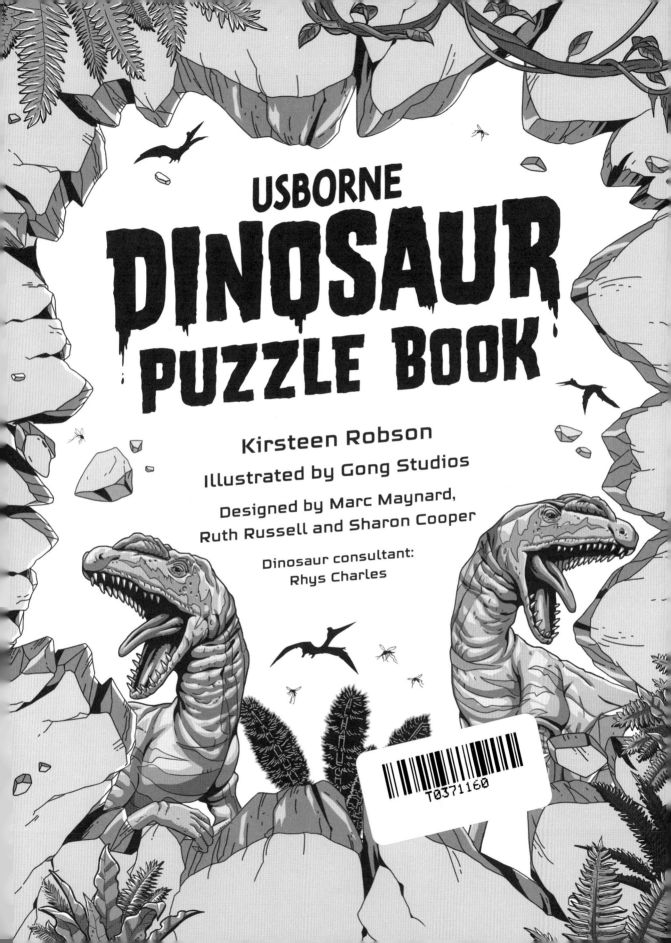

Usborne
DINOSAUR
PUZZLE BOOK

Kirsteen Robson

Illustrated by Gong Studios

Designed by Marc Maynard, Ruth Russell and Sharon Cooper

Dinosaur consultant:
Rhys Charles

T0371160

SHADOW MATCH

Circle the shadow below that belongs to this Stegosaurus.

VICIOUS WEAPON

Stegosaurus used its sturdy tail spikes for protection, swinging them violently at attackers to prevent them from getting too close.

BUGGING YOU

Draw stripes on $\frac{1}{5}$ of these prehistoric bugs, spots on half of the remaining ones, and zigzags on half of the rest. How many remain undecorated?

SPELLING SCRAMBLE

Unscramble the letters below each dinosaur name to see the country where each dinosaur's fossils were first discovered.

Microraptor
HICAN

Spinosaurus
PEGTY

Baryonyx
DANNLEG

T. Rex
MICARAE

Leaellynasaura
ARIATALUS

WORD SMASH

Draw a line to connect the two halves of each dinosaur name on the rocks below.

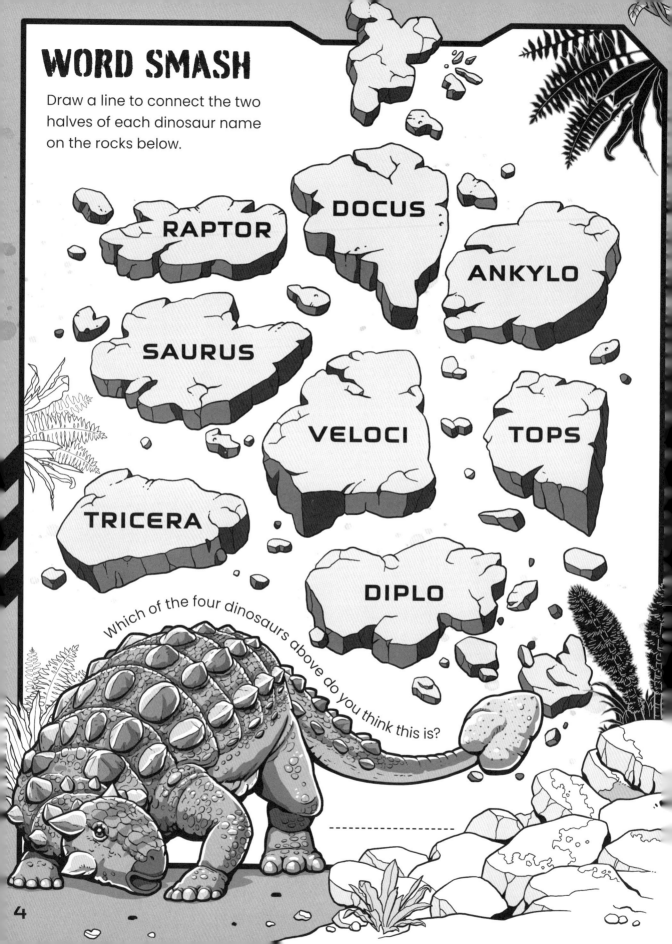

RAPTOR

DOCUS

ANKYLO

SAURUS

VELOCI

TOPS

TRICERA

DIPLO

Which of the four dinosaurs above do you think this is?

_____

DINO-DOKU

Fill in the grid so that all four footprints appear in every row, column and block of four.

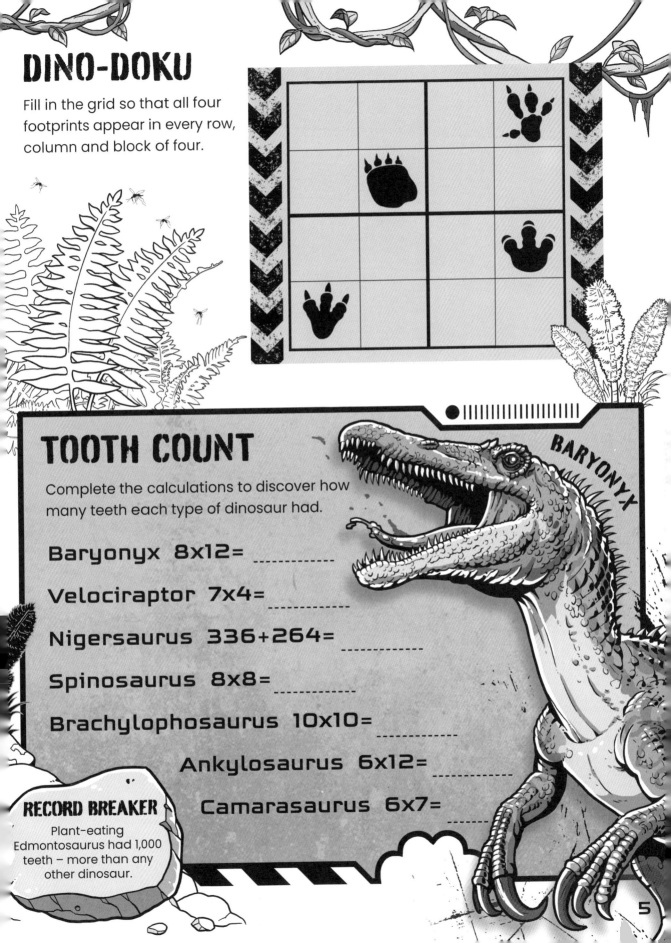

TOOTH COUNT

Complete the calculations to discover how many teeth each type of dinosaur had.

Baryonyx 8x12= _____

Velociraptor 7x4= _____

Nigersaurus 336+264= _____

Spinosaurus 8x8= _____

Brachylophosaurus 10x10= _____

Ankylosaurus 6x12= _____

Camarasaurus 6x7= _____

BARYONYX

RECORD BREAKER

Plant-eating Edmontosaurus had 1,000 teeth – more than any other dinosaur.

SOMETHING FISHY

Lead Spinosaurus through the weedy swamp to catch up with Onchopristis.

ONCHOPRISTIS

DINOSAUR A-Z

Look at the list of dinosaurs below, then see if you can find their names in the grid. They may be written forward or backward in any direction.

EORAPTOR

```
T A U S T E G O C E R A S I Y S N U S N A
A U M T U Y U L V P U S A R U T S R O T G
H E O N A H A G P I R Y A R O I I U J O Z
T T L T L N C M I N R S U I I T R M O A A
A N T P U I O Y Z O C A I T X I P O B P L
S R D R A U A R N I S P P A Y A S A A D M
U H O O A M G T I O X B H T N R G I R A O
L I M T W M P N C O N Q E O O T A G I O X
T E T P P E R A O P J I M R Y R L N A E E
A R U A S A N Y L L E A E L R U L I N T S
O T Q R P I R D N L O T S D A R I M L U O
C E Z I P I F H I I O W T A B Z M O U R S
L O R C T U T O A C P S U S U M I N M I N
A O R O F T C I P T E I A Z R R M I S M E
Z C C L O U E I C H U R P U T P U I I T D
T S I E X K E N T R O S A U R U S S I T A
E N R V T N O T L I R D V T O U R R L X T
U H Y P S I L O P H O D O N O G S S X O I
Q U O Y J D O O U R D O N N D P R N R O U
J C U A S D U X M C S A E I O O S U I L R
T O P C L A F R X U W U L O N G U S O N F
```

ALLOSAURUS
BARYONYX
CITIPATI
DEINONYCHUS
EORAPTOR
FRUITADENS
GALLIMIMUS
HYPSILOPHODON
IRRITATOR

JOBARIA
KENTROSAURUS
LEAELLYNASAURA
MINMI
NOMINGIA
OVIRAPTOR
PINACOSAURUS
QUETZALCOATLUS
RIOJASAURUS

STEGOCERAS
TROODON
UTAHRAPTOR
VELOCIRAPTOR
WENDICERATOPS
XUWULONG
YUTYRANNUS
ZALMOXES

DEINONYCHUS

CLAWS FOR THOUGHT

Draw around the two Utahraptor feet that do not match the others.

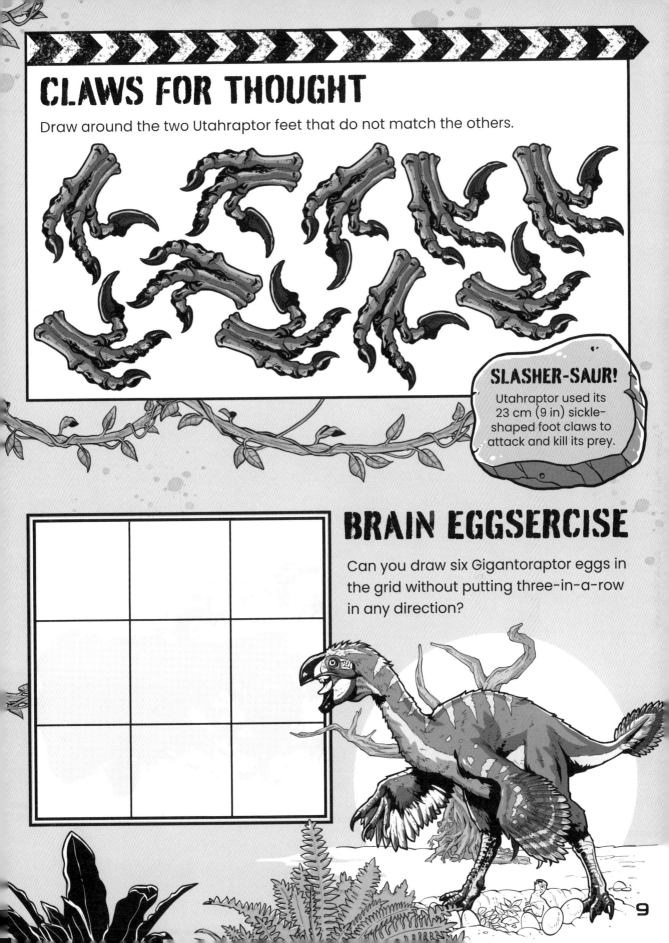

SLASHER-SAUR!

Utahraptor used its 23 cm (9 in) sickle-shaped foot claws to attack and kill its prey.

BRAIN EGGSERCISE

Can you draw six Gigantoraptor eggs in the grid without putting three-in-a-row in any direction?

DINOCUBE

Which of these flat shapes could be cut out and folded to make this dinosaur cube? Circle its letter.

A

B

C

D

Rock  Stop

The unit of currency at Rock Stop Souvenirs is the Rock.

1 Rock = 100 Stones

The price of something that costs 6 Rocks and 30 Stones is written as R6.30. Can you calculate the cost of the things on the shopping list below? Write your answers on the list.

A T-shirt and a pen ----------------------

Two pairs of sunglasses ------------------

One notebook and three pens --------------

Four sticker books ----------------------

STICKERS
R7.00

T. REX T
R12.50

PTERO-PENS
R2.25

STEGOSHADES
R8.70

DI-NOTES
R3.20

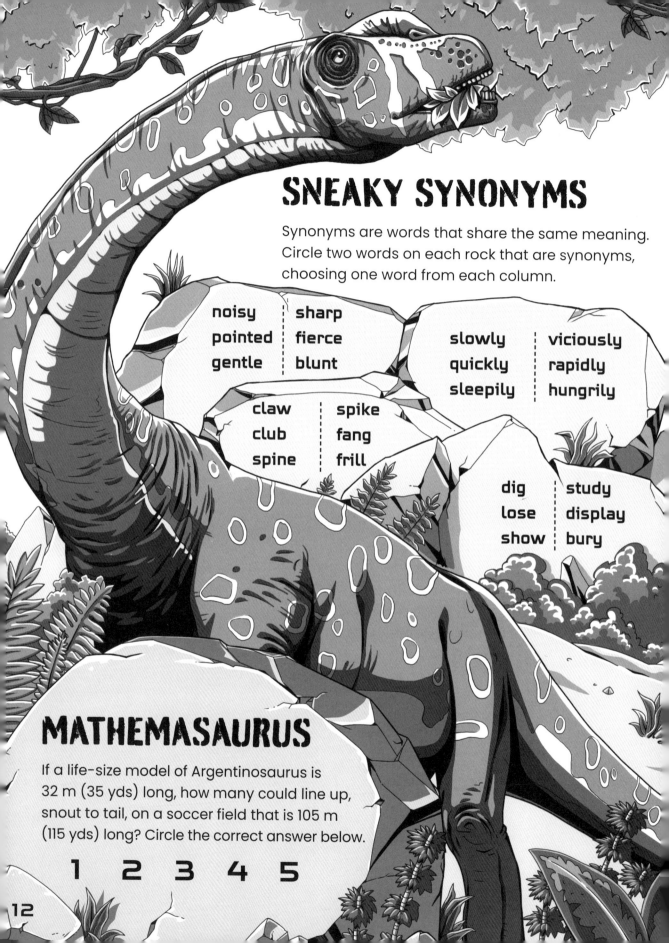

SNEAKY SYNONYMS

Synonyms are words that share the same meaning. Circle two words on each rock that are synonyms, choosing one word from each column.

noisy	sharp
pointed	fierce
gentle	blunt

slowly	viciously
quickly	rapidly
sleepily	hungrily

claw	spike
club	fang
spine	frill

dig	study
lose	display
show	bury

MATHEMASAURUS

If a life-size model of Argentinosaurus is 32 m (35 yds) long, how many could line up, snout to tail, on a soccer field that is 105 m (115 yds) long? Circle the correct answer below.

1   2   3   4   5

TRICKY TRICERATOPS

Can you spot the sequences in each row, adding the missing details to the final picture to complete each sequence?

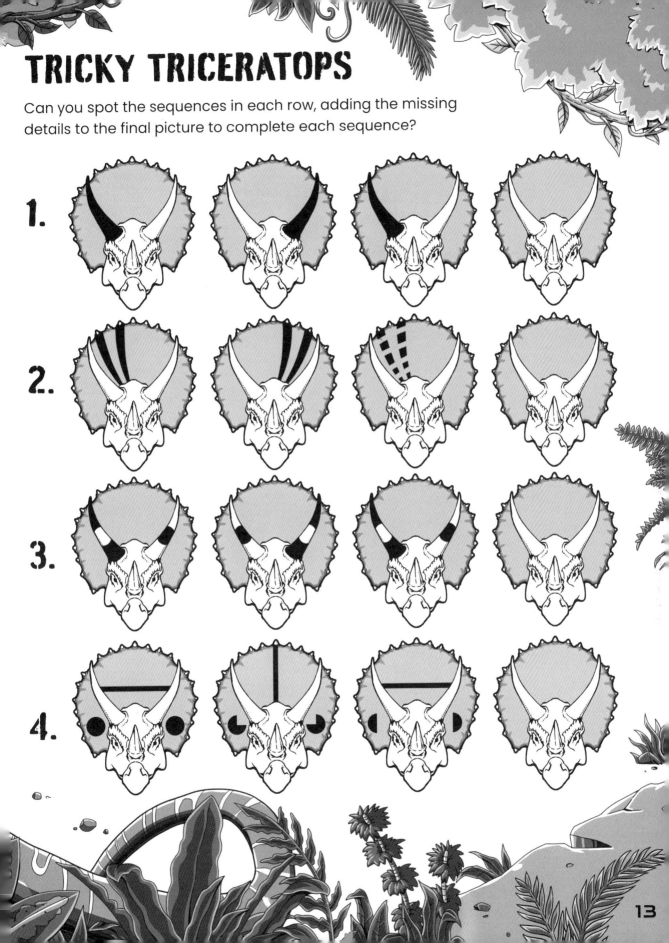

FINISH THE FOSSIL

Use the grid to help you finish this picture of a Trilobite fossil.

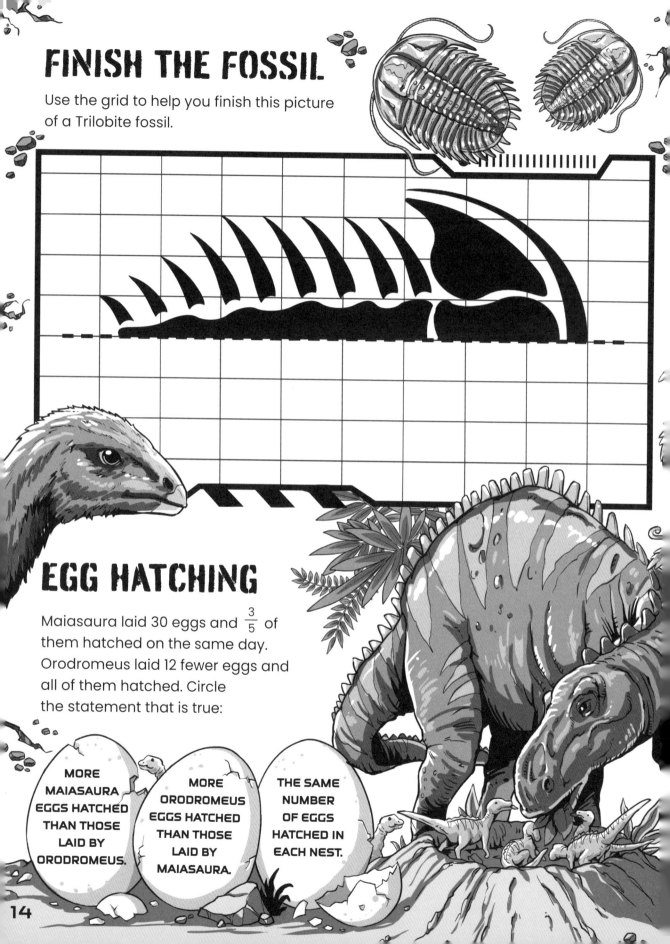

EGG HATCHING

Maiasaura laid 30 eggs and $\frac{3}{5}$ of them hatched on the same day. Orodromeus laid 12 fewer eggs and all of them hatched. Circle the statement that is true:

MORE MAIASAURA EGGS HATCHED THAN THOSE LAID BY ORODROMEUS.

MORE ORODROMEUS EGGS HATCHED THAN THOSE LAID BY MAIASAURA.

THE SAME NUMBER OF EGGS HATCHED IN EACH NEST.

MODEL MIX-UP

Which set of bones from the bottom of the page do you need to build the T. Rex skeleton model below?

ANSWER: _ _ _ _ _ _ _ _ _ _ _ _ _

TERRIFYING TEETH

The longest dinosaur tooth ever found is 30 cm (12 in) long – in a T. Rex skeleton known as Sue.

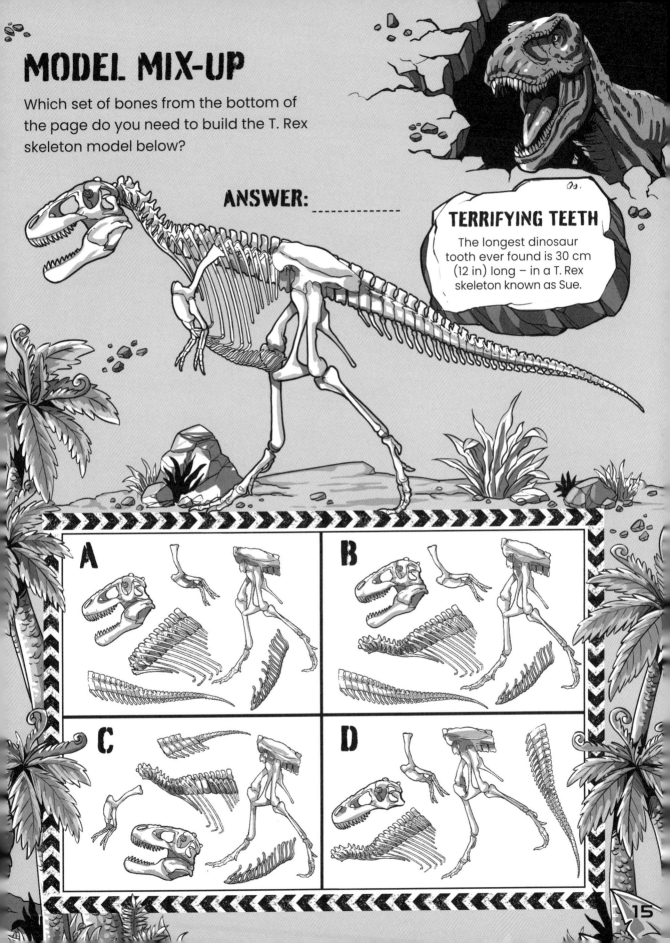

A

B

C

D

WHOSE HEAD?

Use the clues at the bottom of the page to write the correct name below each dinosaur. You'll need to read all the clues first.

CLUES

1. Heterodontosaurus is directly above Baryonyx, which is next to Eoraptor.

2. Sinornithosaurus is on the bottom row.

3. Rugops is directly above Eoraptor and next to Apatosaurus, which is on the left.

4. Zuniceratops is directly above Rugops.

5. Saltasaurus is on the right, on the row above Rugops.

6. Sinosaurus is not on the bottom row.

7. Baryonyx eats fish.

CODE SPOTTER

Use the alphabet to help you crack and use the secret codes below.

ABCDEFGHIJKLMNOPQRSTUVWXYZ

EACH CODE IS DIFFERENT.

17

EXAMPLE

ARM = BSN

Here, each letter is replaced by the one after it in the alphabet. So:

LEG = M F H
      _ _ _

HAMMER = GZLLDQ

_ _ _ _ _ _ = AQTRG

HEAD = JGCF

TAIL = _ _ _ _

FOSSIL = DMQQGJ

_ _ _ _ = PMAI

TURNING FERNS

Circle the fossilized fern that can be rotated to be an exact match of the one below.

Fossilized
fern

DINNER DETECTIVE

Follow the stony paths to discover the kind of food each dinosaur outside the shaded oval ate.

BARYONYX

BRACHYLOPHOSAURUS

AUSTRORAPTOR

GYRODUS

STEGOSAURUS

PROTEA

ORDER, ORDER

Put the dinosaurs below in order – longest to shortest. Write their letters on the correct numbered lines.

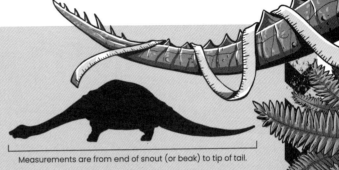

Measurements are from end of snout (or beak) to tip of tail.

A	B	C	D	E
Triceratops	Baryonyx	Stegosaurus	Pteranodon	Diplodocus
9 m (30 ft)	10 m (33 ft)	7 m (23 ft)	2.6 m (8.5 ft)	26 m (85 ft)

1. _____   2. _____   3. _____   4. _____   5. _____

CARNOTAURUS

ROCK EATERS
Some dinosaurs, including Stegosaurus, swallowed stones, which helped grind up food in their stomachs.

VELOCIRAPTOR

PURGATORIUS

FERNS

THREE X THREE

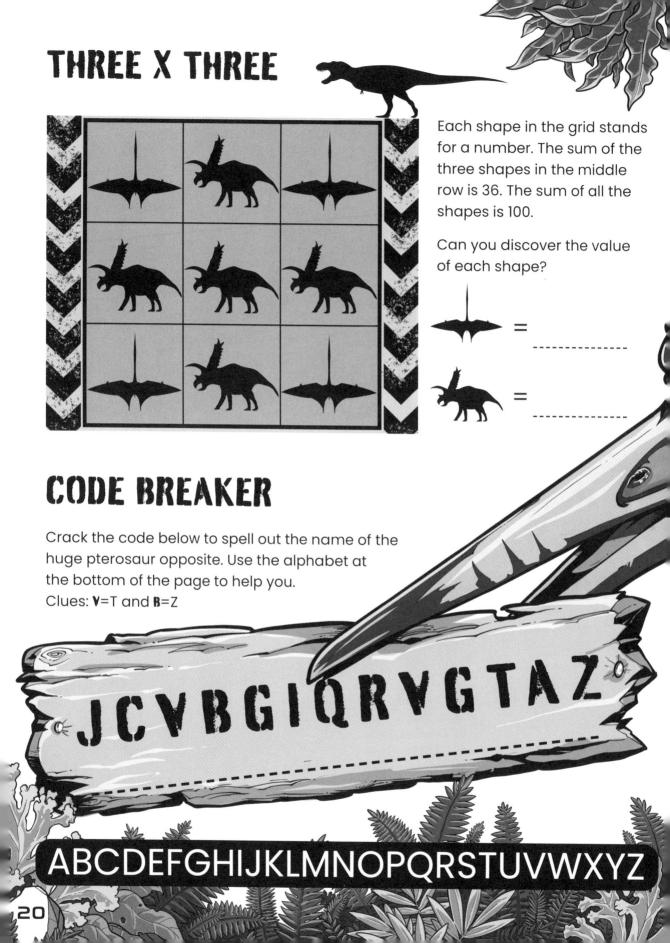

Each shape in the grid stands for a number. The sum of the three shapes in the middle row is 36. The sum of all the shapes is 100.

Can you discover the value of each shape?

= --------------

= --------------

CODE BREAKER

Crack the code below to spell out the name of the huge pterosaur opposite. Use the alphabet at the bottom of the page to help you.

Clues: **V**=T and **B**=Z

JCVBGIQRVGTAZ

ABCDEFGHIJKLMNOPQRSTUVWXYZ

BEGINNINGS AND ENDINGS

Circle the word on each shaded panel below that is related to the words on either side of the panel in the same way as in example A.

A. clap   (claw)   clam   gnat   gnaw

1. tall   torn   tail   mail   sail

2. hole   pole   wail   horn   warn

3. clip   stop   club   clue   stub

BIG WINGS

This pterosaur had a wingspan about three times that of Eurazhdarcho, which was 3.8 m (12.5 ft). About how wide were this creature's wings in total?

CODE CRASH

Use the values on the broken rocks to complete the calculations below.

N=10

R=6

H=5

O=3

$H+O+R-N =$ ☐

$H \times O+R+N =$ ☐

$N \div H \times R+O =$ ☐

$R \div O \times N-H =$ ☐

EGGS IN ORDER

Circle the speckled Oviraptor egg whose number goes next in the sequence below.

1   3   7   13   ?

19   21   23   25

JIXIANGORNIS

SINOSAUROPTERYX

JEHOLORNIS

CAUDIPTERYX

PSITTACOSAURUS

MICRORAPTOR

DINO SWAP

Look at this picture for ten seconds. Then turn the page to spot which animals have changed places.

JIXIANGORNIS

CAUDIPTERYX

JEHOLORNIS

SINOSAUROPTERYX

PSITTACOSAURUS

DINO SWAP

Did you spot who had swapped places? (See the puzzle instruction on page 23.)

MICRORAPTOR

HIDDEN!

Fill in every triangle to see what's hiding here.

SPELLING SHAMBLES

Find and circle seven spelling mistakes on the fact sheet about Caulkicephalus.

CAULKICEPHALUS

Living in the Early Cretaceous period, about 130 milllion years ago, Caulkicefhalus was one of the biggest and last species of pterosaurs too have teeth. It's dagger-like front teeth interlocked to help it spear and trap its slippery fish pray. With a small body and 5 m (16.5 ft) wingspan, it was skilled at soring above the waves or skiming the surface in search of food.

FISH FEAST

Circle the letter of the trail that will lead hungry Elasmosaurus to its Enchodus prey.

SQUARE BUBBLES

Draw a square around each bubble with a square number inside. (4 and 9 are examples of square numbers. 4 = 2 x 2, 9 = 3 x 3...)

DID YOU KNOW?
Elasmosaurus was 14 m (46 ft) long – that's longer than T. Rex.

63

27

81

25

100

49

12

36

35

16

64

ONE STOMP AT A TIME

Circle the footprint from the group of six on the right that goes next in the footprint number sequence below.

12 24 36 48 ?

FOSSIL TRACKS
Preserved dinosaur footprints have their own name – they are known as ichnites (pronounced "ik-nites").

T. REX

58
72
52
60
49
62

DO-YOU-THINK-YOU-SAW-IT?

Unscramble the letters below to discover the names of four dinosaurs.

SOURUSPINAS

DOCSPUDOIL

SASNARYOUTRUN XER

RITCARESPOT

WEIGHT IN LINE

Number the creatures in order from heaviest to lightest. (They're not shown to scale.)

10 kg (22 lb)
Thalassodromeus

350 kg (772 lb)
Herrerasaurus

103 kg (227 lb)
Deinonychus

8 tonnes (8.8 US tons)
Triceratops

2.25 tonnes (2.5 US tons)
Gigantoraptor

55 tonnes (60.6 US tons)
Patagotitan

RAZOR SHARP

Cretoxyrhina had around 48 teeth in its upper jaw and 52 in its lower jaw.

Tylosaurus had up to 26 teeth in its upper jaw, 26 in its lower jaw and 22 others on the roof of its mouth.

Which creature had more teeth?

CRETOXYRHINA

TYLOSAURUS

FLYING HIGH

Draw around the flying Quetzalcoatlus that is the most different from the others.

FLYING GIANTS

With a wingspan of up to 11 m (36 ft), Quetzalcoatlus is thought to be the largest flying creature ever!

CRACKING TIME

What fraction of the total number of eggs are cracked?

ANSWER:

T. REX TROUBLE

Underline the subject of the sentence below. Then circle the adjective and draw zigzags around the verb.

THE FEROCIOUS T. REX HUNGRILY ATTACKED THE TRICERATOPS.

SEEING DOUBLE

Find and draw around the two pictures in this white panel that are not one of a matching pair.

ANCIENT BONES

Fossils of Hadrosaurus were discovered 43 years before remains of Coelophysis. Coelophysis bones were found 182 years after fossils of Megalosaurus. Complete the labels and draw around the label of the fossil that was found in an even-numbered year.

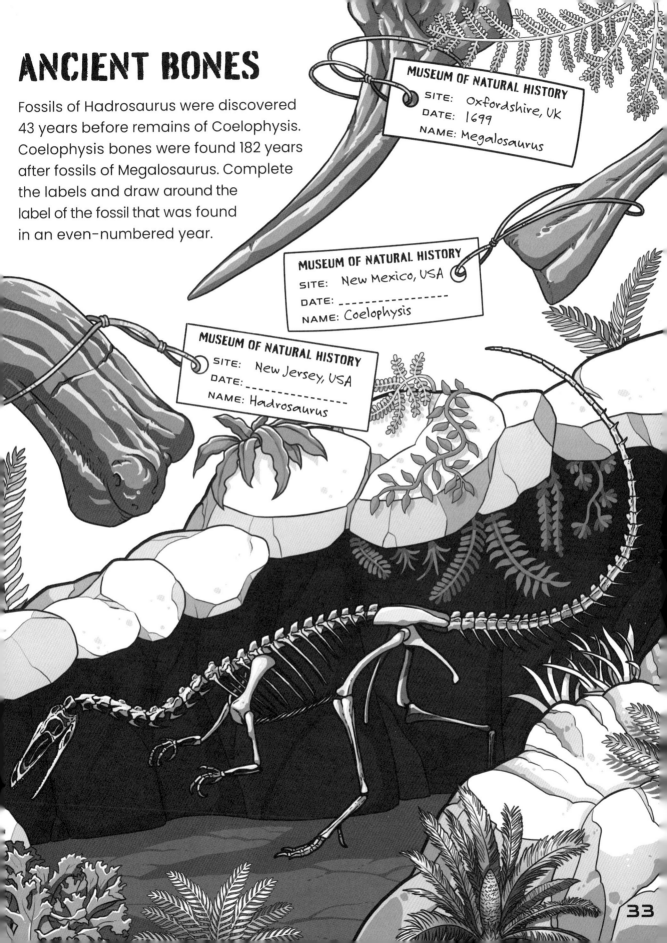

MUSEUM OF NATURAL HISTORY
SITE: Oxfordshire, UK
DATE: 1699
NAME: Megalosaurus

MUSEUM OF NATURAL HISTORY
SITE: New Mexico, USA
DATE: _____
NAME: Coelophysis

MUSEUM OF NATURAL HISTORY
SITE: New Jersey, USA
DATE: _____
NAME: Hadrosaurus

BRAINTEASERS

Unscramble the letters to discover
five objects that are the same sizes
as these dinosaurs' brains.

LUMP

1. ------------------
   STEGOSAURUS

MANUH NIBRA

2. ------------------------
   TYRANNOSAURUS REX

GNIP NOGP ALBL

3. ------------------------
   GALLIMIMUS

ANNABA

4. ------------------------
   GIGANOTOSAURUS

SPOT THE OPPOSITES

Circle the two words (one from each three-word group) that have opposite meanings.

1.

TALL
HEAVY
FIERCE

STRONG
SHORT
LARGE

2.

HUNGRY
AWAKE
NIMBLE

TIRED
ASLEEP
PEACEFUL

3.

SPIKED
HORNED
ROUGH

FEATHERY
SMOOTH
STICKY

4.

DANGEROUS
SECURE
DEAFENING

THREATENING
NOISY
SAFE

WRONG HEADED

An Apatosaurus skeleton was wrongly displayed in a museum for 45 years, with the head of a Camarasaurus.

NUHAM STIF

5. -
APATOSAURUS

SQUARE PIECES

Write an X under each of the two squares at the bottom of the page that will finish the picture of Sauropelta and Deinonychus.

DEINONYCHUS

SAUROPELTA

WINGING IT

If there are 24 Sinaeschnidia dragonflies, each with two pairs of wings, how many wings are there in total? Write your answer in the box below.

You can use this space for your calculations too.

MIRROR, MIRROR

Use the grid to help you draw the other half of the dragonfly picture.

WOW WINGS!

With a wingspan as wide as an adult's arm, the largest known insect of all time was Meganeuropsis, which lived over 30 million years before the first dinosaurs.

MONSTER MEAT-MUNCHERS

Can you fit the names of ten of the biggest meat-eating dinosaurs into the grid below? Start with the longest name then use the letters to figure out which name goes where. The numbers by the grid show the dinosaurs' size order.

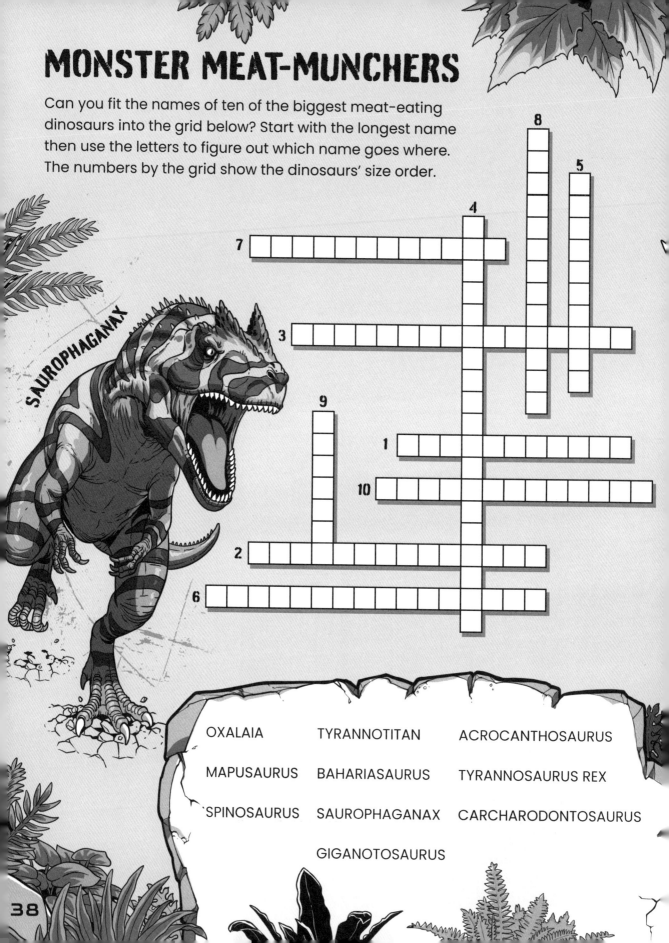

OXALAIA

MAPUSAURUS

SPINOSAURUS

TYRANNOTITAN

BAHARIASAURUS

SAUROPHAGANAX

GIGANOTOSAURUS

ACROCANTHOSAURUS

TYRANNOSAURUS REX

CARCHARODONTOSAURUS

WHEEL OF PTERROR

How many words can you make using the letters in this word wheel? All of the words must include the letter in the middle. (High scorer = 8 words or more)

-------------------- --------------------

-------------------- --------------------

-------------------- --------------------

-------------------- --------------------

PTERANODON

LEAF SEQUENCE

Circle the dark leaf at the bottom of the page that goes next in the number sequence below.

1   4   9   ?

14   15   16   17

SUPER SKULLS

From the tip of its toothless beak to the end of its majestic headcrest, Pteranodon's skull was longer than the whole of the rest of its body.

DASH OF DOOM

Show the Triceratops the way between the streams of lava to the rest of the herd.

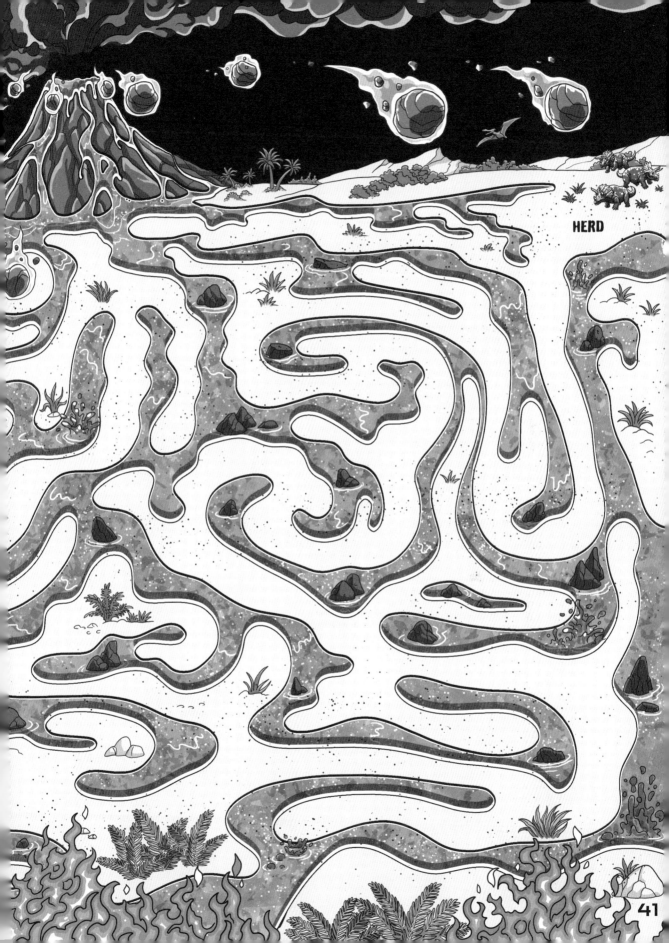

HERD

DINOCHARTS

A group of children voted for the attraction they liked best at a prehistoric theme park and recorded their results in a pictogram.

DRACOREX DUNGEONS	HOOK A HADROSAUR	RIDE THE T. REX CUPS	TOTAL PTERROR!	DIPPY-DIPPER	GHOSTY-SAURUS

How many children enjoyed the Dippy-Dipper ride the most?

- - - - - - - - - - - - -

How many more children liked the T. Rex Cups than the Ghosty-saurus?

- - - - - - - - - - - - -

How many children were in the group?

- - - - - - - - - - - - -

WEIGHTY ROCKS

This pictogram shows the weights of five dinosaurs. Ankylosaurus weighs about 8 tonnes (over 8 US tons).

How much heavier is Apatosaurus than Shantungosaurus?

How much does Ledumahadi weigh?

What is the combined weight of Ledumahadi and Supersaurus?

KEY
= 8 tonnes
(over 8 US tons)

ANKYLOSAURUS	🪨
SHANTUNGOSAURUS	🪨 🪨
LEDUMAHADI	🪨 🪨
SUPERSAURUS	🪨 🪨 🪨 🪨
APATOSAURUS	🪨 🪨 🪨

SHANTUNGOSAURUS

UNDER THE SEA

Connect all the dots that are multiples of three to finish this ammonite. Start at 3, then go up in order.

43

LONG IN THE TOOTH

Draw the other half of each dinosaur tooth shape.

THAT'S NOT MY DINOSAUR!

Draw around the circle below that does not belong to the Yutyrannus picture on the right.

FEATHERY GIANT

Yutyrannus (meaning "feathered tyrant") was one of the largest dinosaur species known to have had feathers.

PAIR ME UP

Circle the word that goes best with **both** pairs of words below.

(RIVER OCEAN) (ICE SNOW)

WINTER

FREEZE

WATER

SWIM

FLOW

D-I-N-O

Fill in the grid so the letters D-I-N-O appear in every row, column and block of four.

D			
	N		
			D
I		O	

LONG-AGO BONES

Write the names of these dinosaurs in date order on the timeline, starting with the one that lived the longest ago and ending with the most recent. ("mya" stands for "million years ago".)

1. _____

ALECTROSAURUS
96 mya
Late Cretaceous period

4. _____

THECODONTOSAURUS
210 mya
Triassic period

5. _____

MONOLOPHOSAURUS
165 mya
Jurassic period

8. _____

CARCHARODONTOSAURUS
99 mya
Late Cretaceous period

2. - - - - - - - - - - - - - - - - -

LYTHRONAX
82 mya
Late Cretaceous period

3. - - - - - - - - - - - - - - - - -

MAJUNGASAURUS
70 mya
Late Cretaceous period

6. - - - - - - - - - - - - - - - - -

LURDUSAURUS
112 mya
Early Cretaceous period

7. - - - - - - - - - - - - - - - - -

IBEROSPINUS
129 mya
Early Cretaceous period

DINO DIG

Which seven things would a fossil scientist be most likely to take on a visit to a hot, dusty desert to dig for dinosaur remains? Write the letters of your chosen items on the list.

Expedition August 23– Sep 17	Items to take with us

COOL CAREER

If you enjoy being outside and are curious about science, geography and Earth's ancient past (including dinosaurs), you might want to train as a palaeontologist*.

*Spelled paleontologist in America.

MONSTER MUNCH

Look at the picture and write down the letter and number of each ammonite's square. Use the key to decode the letters, then use the squares' numbers to help you arrange the letters on the numbered lines below to finish spelling out the name of this hungry predator.

```
          R
 __  __  __  __  __  __  __  __  __  __
 1   2   3   4   5   6   7   8   9  10
```

= Ammonite

KEY

A = R
B = U
C = M
D = E
E = A
F = O
G = S
H = L

Ammonite
A8

10 9 8 7 6 5 4 3 2 1

A B C D E F G H

THE ORB OF DESTINY

Read the story below then answer the questions.

Jed knew it was special as soon as he glimpsed it in the cluttered window of "Crawley's Curiosities". The globe glowed gently, pulsing with an aura of ancient power. Unable to resist, Jed pushed open the heavy door and stepped inside. Minutes later, the boy was back on the dark, snowy

5 street. His ten-year-old hands no longer clutched his birthday money but instead cupped the curves of a smooth sphere. It was the egg (so Mr. Crawley had assured him) of a Saurolophus – a gentle, plant-eating dinosaur giant. Jed's new prized possession felt strangely warm in his palm. Hardly daring to breathe, he slowly stroked the silky shell.

10 Barely had his finger begun to move when he was pulled violently backward, as though invisible ropes were wrapped around his waist. The wind whistled past his cheeks, his blood pounded in his ears and his head spun as he hurtled along a snaking tunnel of whirling dust, swirling darkness and

15 dazzling light. Shutting his eyes in terror, he hugged the egg to his chest and longed for the sickening journey to end.

Bam! Jed's back slammed into something hard and he crumpled to the ground. He lay there for a while, gasping in great gulps of air, giddy with relief that his ordeal was over. But as his own breathing eased, he was aware of a stronger,

20 warmer breeze slowly sucking and blowing across his entire body. A rotting stench filled his nostrils. Filled with dread, he unscrewed his eyes to find himself staring into the gaping maw of a living, breathing dinosaur. But this was not Saurolophus. This was a creature far, far more terrible and it was not expecting leaves for lunch...

1. **What time of year does this story take place?**

   A A spring morning

   B A summer afternoon

   C A September evening

   D A winter afternoon

2. **Why was Jed "hardly daring to breathe" as he stroked the egg (line 9)?**

   A He was excited something might happen.

   B He had a cold and didn't want to cough.

   C He was frightened of warming the egg.

   D He had hiccups.

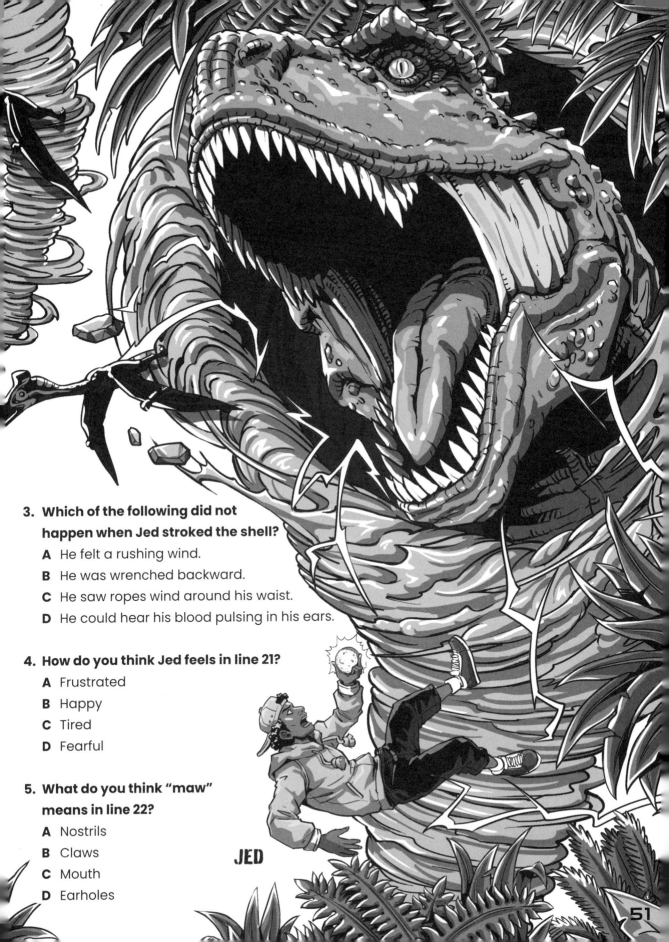

3. **Which of the following did not happen when Jed stroked the shell?**
   - **A** He felt a rushing wind.
   - **B** He was wrenched backward.
   - **C** He saw ropes wind around his waist.
   - **D** He could hear his blood pulsing in his ears.

4. **How do you think Jed feels in line 21?**
   - **A** Frustrated
   - **B** Happy
   - **C** Tired
   - **D** Fearful

5. **What do you think "maw" means in line 22?**
   - **A** Nostrils
   - **B** Claws
   - **C** Mouth
   - **D** Earholes

JED

DINO DRAW

Five friends entered a drawing competition. You can see their pictures here. Alba was placed before Bai but behind Cathal. Ellis came before Devin but behind Bai.

ALBA

CATHAL

BAI

DEVIN

ELLIS

Figure out the order of prizes and write the correct names on the certificates.

DINO DRAW
1st Prize

DINO DRAW
2nd Prize

DINO DRAW
3rd Prize

DINO DRAW
4th Prize

DINO DRAW
5th Prize

DINO DIFFERENCES

Spot ten differences between the pictures below, showing T. Rex with a pair of Dakotaraptors.

DINO CODE CRUNCH

Look at the three words and the three numbers below. Crack the code to find out which digit belongs to each letter, then answer the questions to finish solving the puzzle.

TIP

Notice the position of repeated letters (such as A) in the words and repeated digits (such as 2) in the numbers.

KEY

A = ____
H = ____
I = ____
L = ____
N = ____
O = ____
R = ____
S = ____
T = ____

LILIENSTERNUS

LASH
HORN
TAIL

3284
5169
4275

What does the code **31135** mean?

What's the code for **Talon**?

LEAF COUNT

How many fossilized Ginkgo leaves are there below?

Ginkgo leaf shape

ANSWER:

PARASAUROLOPHUS PUZZLER

Fit all the numbers 1 to 9 into the grid below, so that the numbers in each row, column and diagonal line of three add up to 15. Three of the numbers have already been filled in for you.

8		
	5	
	7	

PARASAUROLOPHUS

HONK! PARP! TOOT!

Once thought to have been a snorkel for underwater breathing, Parasaurolophus's head crest more likely helped it to make honking sounds to communicate with the rest of the herd.

NEXT IN LINE

Circle the shape on the right of each box that goes next in each sequence.

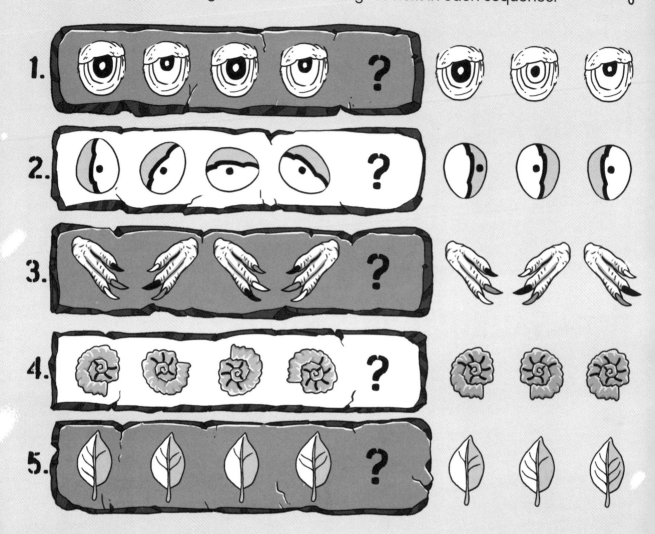

TAILOR-MADE

Leaellynasaura's tail may have been over 2 times as long as the rest of its body.

1. If a young Leaellynasaura's tail was 30 cm (12 in), how long was its body in total?

UNDER _____

2. If an adult Leaellynasaura was 0.9 m (3 ft) in total, how long was its tail?

OVER _____

HOW MANY ERRORS?

Circle the mistakes in your friend's homework and give a score out of 25, subtracting half a point for each error.

My projekt about dinosaur's

My favurite dinosaur was fist discoverd in a place known as Dinasaur Cove in australia.

It was named Leaellynasaura after leaellyn Rich, the daughter of the Austrailian palyontologists who found the fosils

when Leaellynasaura was alive Australia was connected to Antarctica. It was not as cold as the Antartic is now but was still a harsh place to suvive in the winter.

SNUGGLY SCARF

Leaellynasaura may have curled its long tail around itself to keep warm as it sheltered in its burrow during the long winter months.

HOW MUCH?

The neck of this Savannasaurus is twice the height of its body, which is 3 m (9.8 ft).

What is the total height of the dinosaur?

Each of this Meganeura's wings is 34 cm (13.39 in) long.

What is the distance across a pair of outstretched wings?

This cycad plant is 625 cm (246 in) tall.

How tall is it in m?	**How tall is it in feet?**
-----------	-----------

This Ankylosaurus weighs 30 times as much as its tail club, which is 20 kg (about 44 lb).

What is the total weight of the dinosaur?

SAVANNASAURUS

MEGANEURA

1 m = 100 cm
1 ft = 12 in

CYCAD

ANKYLOSAURUS

WHO'S WHO?

Can you write the correct dinosaur name on each fact card? You can use the page numbers to find useful clues to help you.

BARYONYX
DIPLODOCUS
PARASAUROLOPHUS
SPINOSAURUS
STEGOSAURUS
TRICERATOPS
T. REX
VELOCIRAPTOR

DINO NAME:

Name meaning: near crested lizard

Length: 10 m (33 ft)
Hip height: 3.5 m (11.5 ft)
Weight: 1.8 tonnes (2 US tons)
Food: conifers, seeds, fruit
Lived: 80–73 mya
Fossils: N.America, Asia

Did you know: May have used its head crest to make trombone-like sounds to signal to its herd.

Page 55

DINO NAME:

Name meaning: heavy claw

Length: 10 m (33 ft)
Hip height: 2.5 m (8.25 ft)
Weight: 1.7 tonnes (1.9 US tons)
Food: fish, dinosaurs
Lived: 130–127 mya
Fossils: UK, Spain, N.Africa

Did you know: Speared fish with hook-like claws and devoured them with its thin, pointed teeth.

Page 18

DINO NAME:

Name meaning: roof lizard

Length: 7 m (23 ft)
Hip height: 2.75 m (9 ft)
Weight: 1.8 tonnes (2 US tons)
Food: leaves
Lived: 156–151 mya
Fossils: USA, Portugal

Did you know: This dinosaur was bigger than an elephant but had a brain the size of a plum.

Page 34

DINO NAME:

Name meaning: three-horned face

Length: 9 m (30 ft)
Hip height: 2 m (7 ft)
Weight: 8 tonnes (8.8 US tons)
Food: ferns, shrubs
Lived: 67–65 mya
Fossils: N.America

Did you know: Was hunted by the most famous killer dinosaur – Tyrannosaurus Rex.

Page 29

DINO NAME:

Name meaning: double beam

Length: 26 m (85 ft)
Hip height: 5 m (16.4 ft)
Weight: 14.8 tonnes (16.3 US tons)
Food: conifer needles
Lived: 154–152 mya
Fossils: USA

Did you know: May have used its long, whip-like tail to make a cracking sound to scare its enemies.

Page 19

DINO NAME:

Name meaning: spine lizard

Length: 16 m (52.5 ft)
Hip height: 4.5 m (14.75 ft)
Weight: 5.5 tonnes (6 US tons)
Food: fish, dinosaurs
Lived: 96–94 mya
Fossils: Egypt, Morocco

Did you know: This largest known of all meat-eating dinosaurs had a spiny sail on its back.

Page 3

DINO NAME:

Name meaning: swift thief

Length: 1.5 m (5 ft)
Hip height: 1 m (3.25 ft)
Weight: 15 kg (33 lb)
Food: Protoceratops
Lived: 125 mya
Fossils: China

Did you know: This fast-running, ferocious predator had 28 teeth; a human adult has 32.

Page 5

DINO NAME:

Name meaning: tyrant lizard king

Length: 12 m (40 ft)
Hip height: 5.5 m (18 ft)
Weight: 6 tonnes (6.6 US tons)
Food: Ceratopsians
Lived: 67–64 mya
Fossils: N.America

Did you know: Longest dinosaur tooth ever found (30 cm (12 in) long) belonged to this creature.

Page 15

PREHISTORIC QUIZ

1. **A Tyrannosaurus was as heavy as a:**

   A Car   **B** Bus   **C** Plane

2. **Young pterosaurs are known as:**

   A Dactylets

   B Wingsters

   C Flaplings

3. **This is a Therizinosaurus, the dinosaur with the longest claws. They were roughly as long as:**

   A A carving knife

   B A tennis racket

   C A golf club

4. **A Diplodocus ate by:**

   A Sucking leaves from branches

   B Raking its teeth along branches

   C Pulling leaves from branches with its tongue

5. **What is a coprolite?**

   A A fossilized dinosaur dropping

   B A hadrosaur's head crest

   C An ankylosaur's tail club

6. **The dinosaur below is a Tylocephale. It had a very high and wide forehead. Its name means:**

   A Swelling head

   B Dome top

   C Thick-head lizard

7. **Which is the correct order for these prehistoric time periods?**

   A Jurassic, Cretaceous, Triassic

   B Cretaceous, Triassic, Jurassic

   C Triassic, Jurassic, Cretaceous

8. **If humans had lived alongside dinosaurs which dinosaur would likely have been the deadliest to people?**

   A Triceratops

   B Utahraptor

   C T. Rex

9. **When the first Triceratops fossil was discovered in 1887, it was thought to be a giant prehistoric:**

   A Goat   **B** Rhino   **C** Bison

10. **Do dinosaur bones have growth rings like tree rings, that form at the rate of one ring a year?**

    A Yes   **B** No

ANSWERS

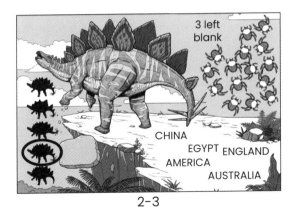

3 left blank

CHINA

EGYPT ENGLAND

AMERICA

AUSTRALIA

2-3

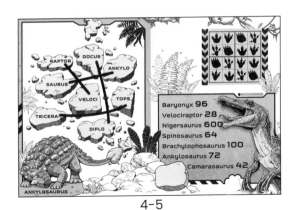

Baryonyx 96
Velociraptor 28
Nigersaurus 600
Spinosaurus 64
Brachylophosaurus 100
Ankylosaurus 72
Camarasaurus 42

4-5

6-7

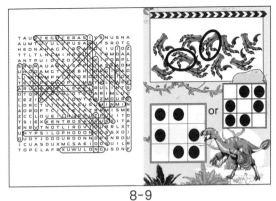

or

8-9

D

R14.75
R17.40
R9.95
R28.00

10-11

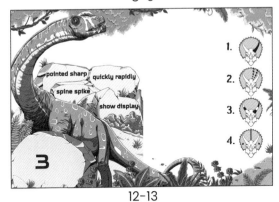

pointed sharp   quickly rapidly

spine spike

show display

3

1.
2.
3.
4.

12-13

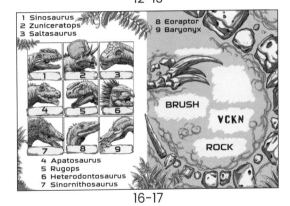

B

14-15

1 Sinosaurus
2 Zuniceratops
3 Saltasaurus

8 Eoraptor
9 Baryonyx

BRUSH

VCKN

ROCK

4 Apatosaurus
5 Rugops
6 Heterodontosaurus
7 Sinornithosaurus

16-17

ANSWERS

18–19

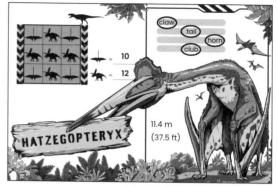

20–21

22–23

24–25

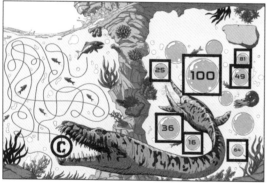

26–27

28–29

30–31

32–33

1. TALL – SHORT
2. AWAKE – ASLEEP
3. ROUGH – SMOOTH
4. DANGEROUS – SAFE

PLUM
HUMAN BRAIN
PING PONG BALL
BANANA
HUMAN FIST

34–35

96 wings

36–37

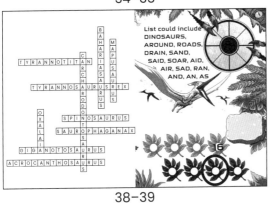

List could include
DINOSAURS,
AROUND, ROADS,
DRAIN, SAND,
SAID, SOAR, AID,
AIR, SAD, RAN,
AND, AN, AS

TYRANNOTITAN
BAHARIASAURA
CARCHARODONTOSAURUS
MAPUSAURUS
TYRANNOSAURUS REX
OXALAIA
SPINOSAURUS
SAUROPHAGANAX
GIGANOTOSAURUS
ACROCANTHOSAURUS

38–39

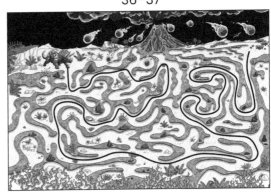

40–41

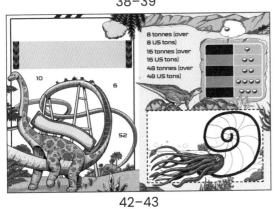

8 tonnes (over 8 US tons)
16 tonnes (over 16 US tons)
48 tonnes (over 48 US tons)

10
6
52

42–43

WATER

DINO
ONDI
NOID
IDON

44–45

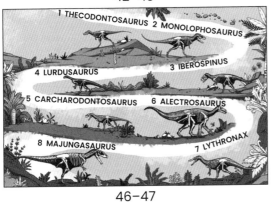

1 THECODONTOSAURUS
2 MONOLOPHOSAURUS
3 IBEROSPINUS
4 LURDUSAURUS
5 CARCHARODONTOSAURUS
6 ALECTROSAURUS
7 LYTHRONAX
8 MAJUNGASAURUS

46–47

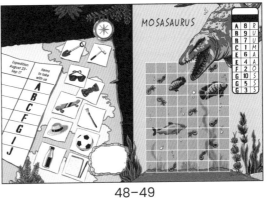

MOSASAURUS

48–49

63

ANSWERS

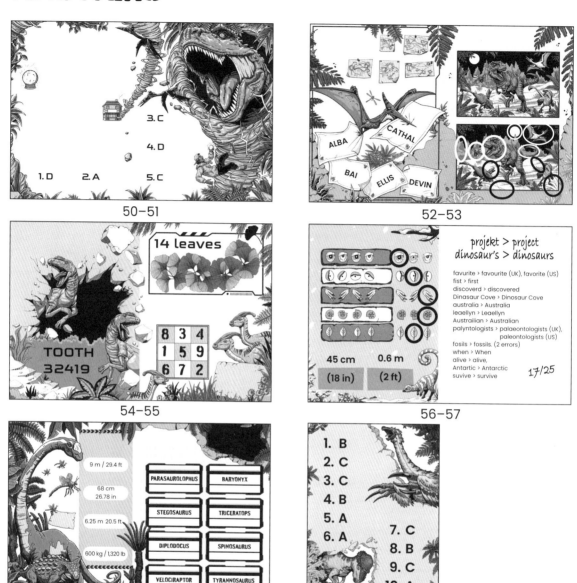

50–51

3. C

4. D

1. D 2. A 5. C

52–53

ALBA CATHAL BAI ELLIS DEVIN

54–55

14 leaves

TOOTH 32419

8	3	4
1	5	9
6	7	2

56–57

projekt > project
dinosaur's > dinosaurs

favurite > favourite (UK), favorite (US)
fist > first
discoverd > discovered
australia > Australia
Dinasaur Cove > Dinosaur Cove
leaellyn > Leaellyn
Austrailian > Australian
palyntologists > palaeontologists (UK),
                 paleontologists (US)
fosils > fossils. (2 errors)
when > When
alive > alive,
Antartic > Antarctic
suvive > survive

45 cm 0.6 m
(18 in) (2 ft)

17/25

58–59

9 m / 29.4 ft

68 cm 26.78 in

6.25 m 20.5 ft

600 kg / 1,320 lb

PARASAUROLOPHUS | BARYONYX

STEGOSAURUS | TRICERATOPS

DIPLODOCUS | SPINOSAURUS

VELOCIRAPTOR | TYRANNOSAURUS REX

60

1. B
2. C
3. C
4. B
5. A
6. A
7. C
8. B
9. C
10. A

Back cover illustration by Franco Tempesta

First published in 2024 by Usborne Publishing Limited,
83-85 Saffron Hill, London EC1N 8RT, United Kingdom. usborne.com